ESSENTIAL LISTENING SKILLS
FOR BUSY SCHOOL STAFF

ESSENTIAL
Listening Skills
for Busy School Staff

What to Say When You Don't Know What to Say

NICK LUXMOORE

Jessica Kingsley *Publishers*
London and Philadelphia

First published in 2015
by Jessica Kingsley Publishers
73 Collier Street
London N1 9BE, UK
and
400 Market Street, Suite 400
Philadelphia, PA 19106, USA

www.jkp.com

Library of Congress Cataloging in Publication Data
A CIP catalog record for this book is available
from the Library of Congress

British Library Cataloguing in Publication Data
A CIP catalogue record for this book is available from the British Library

ISBN 978 1 84905 565 9
eISBN 978 1 78450 000 9

Printed and bound in Great Britain

MIX
Paper from
responsible sources
FSC
www.fsc.org   FSC® C013056

CONTENTS

ACKNOWLEDGEMENTS

I'm grateful to Julia Peto, Fiona Luxmoore, Debbie Lee, Kathy Peto and to staff at King Alfred's Academy, Wantage, for reading and commenting on earlier drafts of this book; to my supervisor, Jane Campbell, and to the other people who listen to me, especially Kathy, Frances and Julia. This book is dedicated to the memory of my father, Rt. Revd. Christopher Luxmoore, who listened to lots of people.

1 INTRODUCTION

You work in a school. It might be a small primary or large secondary school. You might be a form tutor, keen to get to know your students, or a classroom teacher, noticing certain behaviours and wondering how best to respond. You might be a teaching assistant, trusted by children who are always telling you things, or one of the receptionists in whom parents and members of staff confide. You might be a playground supervisor, librarian, matron, caretaker, secretary, bursar, cook, cleaner, lab or computer technician. You might be the headteacher... Whatever your job, people talk to you, telling you things about themselves and needing you to listen. And you do listen, but there isn't always time and, in any case, it's hard to know what to say sometimes, how best to help people who are struggling.

This book is for you. You'll be busy in school with umpteen things to do, people to see, places to be. You'll be good at your job and will want your school to succeed, but nowhere in your job description will it say anything about the importance of listening to other people. Listening will be taken for granted as something that you do all the time. It'll be the glue holding (or not holding) your school together, because everyone knows that the headteacher can come up with great plans: what makes those plans work, what makes the school feel like a creative or uncreative, supportive or unsupportive place will be the quality of the relationships between people and the extent to which those people are able to support each other through the daily – sometimes hourly – business of helping when someone's down, when they're feeling angry or sad or feeling that they don't matter.

This book is about becoming more confident and effective in that daily work of listening, listening, listening. It's a book about the different kinds of listening you're obliged to do and about what exactly it is that you're listening for. It's about what to say when you don't know what to say and about how to listen when there's never enough time.

As professionals, we regularly find ourselves listening to children and young people. But we might equally well find ourselves listening to colleagues, and sometimes we'll find ourselves listening to parents. This book is about responding to all these people: an angry parent in reception; a teacher in tears in the staffroom; a student making threats in the corridor... You might be the person responding to these visible signs of distress or you might be elsewhere at the time, holding things together through the daily work of respecting, appreciating and listening to people because you know that unless this work is going on in the background, there'll be more and more angry parents in reception, more and more teachers in tears, more and more students making threats, cutting themselves, misbehaving, under-achieving, staying at home...

It's easy to feel overwhelmed by the neediness of other people, and tempting to avoid the really heavy stuff by dishing out quick advice, hoping that it'll do for the time being. It's tempting to put up the barricades, insisting, 'We're not paid to deal with this stuff! Teachers are here to teach and students are here to learn!' Yet every member of staff knows that learning is powerfully affected by the prevailing atmosphere in the school and by the quality of the relationships between people. The inspectors know this too. When they come calling, they want to know about more than just exam results; they want to know about how the people involved in the school (students, staff and parents) are feeling: whether these people feel heard, whether they feel safe, whether their concerns are responded to and taken seriously, whether relationships between people are respectful or whether, instead, there's bullying, harassment and discrimination. Some schools invite students to put their written concerns into confidential boxes; they devise surveys to elicit the views of staff and they arrange forums for parents to say what they're thinking. These initiatives all have their place, but the fact of their existence doesn't mean that anyone necessarily feels heard or respected or safe.

The more effectively we're able to listen, the more people will be able to get on with their school lives without other things getting in their way. **When they don't feel heard, people end up acting out their feelings in order to be heard and their actions often have unfortunate consequences:** the angry girl ends up swearing at her teacher; the lonely teacher stops coming to school; the despairing parent takes it out on the child. Adults may be more subtle but are just as capable as children and young people of turning their feelings into disruptive behaviour of one sort or another. With children and young people we can respond with behaviour plans, but a behaviour plan is only ever as effective as the listening that went into understanding the behaviour in the first place, and only as effective as the listening that sustains the plan once things start to go awry.

Listening to another person sounds simple, and sometimes it is. But at other times it gets complicated. We fill up with feelings ourselves; we worry about saying the wrong thing or missing the point; we worry about not being able to help, about making things worse. This book is about what we *can* do and what *is* possible when we listen and try to understand other people. It's not about immediately suggesting that the other person would be better off talking to a counsellor or doctor, to somebody from an outside agency or, simply, to a more senior member of staff. In pointing people towards these 'experts' rather than listening ourselves, there's a danger of implying that the person in need is somehow beyond our comprehension when, in fact, he or she will be neither mad nor bad but simply another human being feeling angry or sad, alone or afraid.

Feeling understood is what most powerfully precipitates change in human beings. Experts are all very well, but understanding our fellow human beings is everyone's potential expertise. Once we start believing that, as mere humans, we're incapable of understanding each other, we're on a slippery slope. Your school may well employ a counsellor or use other 'experts' to help with specific problems. Having access to professionals like these is great but it's the quality of *everyone's* listening that makes the real difference. Most people will never make an appointment to see a counsellor, but that won't stop them wanting to talk about their lives, about how they're feeling, about what happened last night or at the weekend. They'll be hoping that their friends in the classroom or staffroom will listen, but sometimes they'll deliberately choose to talk with people who aren't necessarily friends, hoping that these people will be better placed to understand. Sometimes they'll want to talk *about* their friends or about what's happening at home, about things from the past or about what might be going to happen next week. The big problem is that, because listening is taken for granted in schools, we find ourselves with little structured time set aside for listening during the school day, and most professionals in schools were never explicitly trained as listeners anyway. Once they've finished their training, all teachers are assumed to be good listeners, as if knowing a lot about History or being skilled at planning a Science lesson automatically qualifies you as a good listener. Listening tends to be seen as a 'soft' rather than as a critical, core skill upon which so much of school life depends. For example, you go to see the headteacher towards the end of a long term. She's usually busy but, on this occasion, welcomes you with a smile, which is encouraging because you haven't actually made an appointment to see her: you were simply hoping that she might be free for a few minutes.

She listens as you tell her how angry you're feeling about various things. She tells you what you should do about each of these things and, a few minutes later, you leave her office. Walking away down the corridor, you notice that you're still feeling angry and wonder why. You realize that it's because you don't feel that she listened – not properly. You didn't need her advice. If you'd needed advice, you'd have asked for it. Rather, you needed her to know how you were feeling and now, instead of feeling better for feeling understood, you've come away feeling like a rather foolish child who's just wasted a grown-up's time. For some reason, your anger made the headteacher defensive, and her defensiveness made her start prescribing solutions rather than listening.

But headteachers are extremely busy people. No one has hours to spend listening to other people's problems. So when you're busy and have only got a few minutes, what *do* you say to a colleague who tells you that he's feeling angry about work? Or suicidal at home? What do you say to another colleague who says she hates her job? How do you listen to the boy in your class whose mother is dying? Or to the girl who's feeling worthless? How do you respond to a boy who feels like giving up? Or to a girl who's so angry that she's threatening to hit someone? What do you say when you're with a parent who can't stop crying? Or when you're on the phone to another parent who's blaming you and the school for everything?

I've worked in schools for over 35 years as a teacher, youth worker, project leader and counsellor. During that time I've run countless training courses for staff, with listening skills usually at the heart of whatever we've been doing together. This book draws on that experience and on my experience as another professional working with so many others in schools, all of us trying to make a difference.

2 YES, BUT…

THERE'S NEVER ENOUGH TIME!

There's a clatter of canteen cutlery up ahead and you're waiting in the queue next to a student you know. Innocently you ask, 'How are you?'

'Not good,' comes the reply.

Now what? Do you ask more, knowing that you only came to buy a quick sandwich because you're already late for something else? Do you pretend not to hear? Do you mumble something like 'Ah well, never mind!' or make a trite remark about everybody's lives being difficult at this time of year?

It's better not to ask the question in the first place if you don't want to know or haven't got time to listen. If you're going to ask, then be prepared to stop and listen, if only for a few minutes. **Good listening isn't about how much time you've got. What matters is the quality rather than**

the quantity of your time. Of course you'd like more time, but a good, uninterrupted four minutes is better than forty minutes of being distracted and trying to do other things at the same time as listening. If necessary, be clear. 'I've got four minutes before I need to be somewhere else.' People will often cut to the chase if they know that there's not much time, or they'll censor themselves, holding on to whatever's troubling them, knowing that they'll need longer than four minutes to do justice to their story.

You might be tidying things away at the end of the day when a colleague sidles over and asks, 'Have you got a minute?'

If you haven't got a minute, it's better to say so in the nicest possible way. And if you do have a minute, then be clear exactly how long that 'minute' can last. 'Yes, I've got three minutes but then I've got to be at a meeting.'

'Ah well, it's nothing important,' says your colleague, retreating. 'I just wanted a chat.'

'Anything in particular?'

'Just life!' she smiles, hesitating. 'Things haven't been too good lately.'

Hearing this, you know that you won't be able to do justice to the conversation in the remaining two and a half minutes before you have to be at your meeting. But at the same time it's important to acknowledge that you've heard what's just been said.

'That sounds really important,' you say. 'There isn't time to talk now, but how about we meet tomorrow at break time?'

There are schools where the only way to get attention is by shouting loudly. Students do it by misbehaving; parents do it by storming into the headteacher's office; colleagues do it by losing their tempers or by bursting into tears or by not coming to school. In schools like these, there's an unspoken belief that waiting patiently to be noticed and heard never works and that distress has to be enacted for anyone to notice. In schools like these, a culture develops where everyone seems perpetually stressed and the days seem to lurch from crisis to crisis. The corridors are full of people running and shouting, pushing past each other. Even the bell seems to ring particularly loudly!

It's important to develop a culture where it's normal for people to get heard but not by shouting louder than anyone else. In a listening culture, running out of lessons in tears doesn't work, and throwing furniture around doesn't work. Asking and arranging to talk with someone, on the other hand, *does* work because everyone in school is a confident listener and everyone in school makes time to listen. 'But not right now. Not when I'm in the middle of doing something else. Let's arrange a time…'

In school, time spent listening has to be boundaried, partly because the listeners are busy people who don't have much time and partly because, even when people are distressed, they have to learn to wait their turn.

'I've got a couple of minutes and then I've got to make a phone call. I know that's not much time, but if we need longer, we can arrange to meet again and carry on talking.'

Once people believe that they'll get heard eventually ('It might not be now and it might not be today but you *will* get your time!'), they learn to wait. That way, anxieties are contained; setbacks don't have to become catastrophes; misfortunes don't have to become tragedies.

There are hit-and-run merchants, however, who drop bombshells knowing full well that there isn't time to talk properly. A girl tells you that she might be pregnant, for example, just as the bell's about to go for the end of the lesson. Or a colleague gets into his car, turns on the engine and tells you through the window – tearfully – that he split up with his partner last night. Sometimes people tell us these things and then run off, in effect, avoiding the conversation, leaving us with the very feelings of helplessness, uselessness and frustration that they themselves are feeling. These feelings don't belong to us but get dumped on us.

What to do? While we always respond to children and young people in real danger, it's important with hit-and-run merchants *not* to over-react by stopping whatever you're doing. After all, boundaries are inevitable, rules are rules and lessons have to continue, even when people are in distress. There are people who will deliberately tell you things when there isn't time to talk because, really, they're testing the boundaries, seeing whether they're special, whether you'll be able to make an exception for them and stop whatever it is that you're doing. They have to learn that they're important, special even, but that your life doesn't necessarily revolve around them.

Sometimes people can't help regressing, especially if that behaviour gets them more time. Claire is fifteen years old but sounds like a five-year-old. 'Everybody hates me!' she says pitifully.

Telling her that she sounds like a five-year-old won't help one little bit. The fact is that we *all* have times when we temporarily become five-year-olds, when the world suddenly seems to be against us, when those old, childlike feelings take hold and we no longer know what to say or do for the best. 'Everybody hates me!' is a way of simplifying life. It might disguise Claire's own hating of other people by making her out to be the poor victim or it might disguise her need to be loved by everyone. 'If I can't be loved by everyone, then I might as well be hated,' she might be saying, in effect. 'At least that way I'll get noticed!'

At times like these, it's important to remember that Claire really *is* (temporarily) a five-year-old, so reasoning with her won't help, punishing her won't help, sarcasm won't help. Only time will dissolve the wave of despair and helplessness washing over her. In a few hours, the five-year-old will transform herself into a fifteen-year-old again.

'Everybody hates me! They're always picking on me! And now other people have started as well!'

'That must be horrible…'

'It is!'

'I'm really sorry…'

'So am I! And there's nothing I can do about it!'

'No, I don't suppose there is…'

This is called a 'paradoxical injunction'. Claire expects you to offer her practical advice because then, every time you suggest something, she can tell you all the reasons why it won't work and why life really *is* as hopeless as she says. So by agreeing with her that life is hopeless, you're changing the roles, taking away her role as the poor victim. Now she may well counter *your* apparent defeatism by suggesting to you a way of changing the situation.

However old we are, taking responsibility for our lives can be frightening. Often, it's better to sympathize with people about how difficult their lives are feeling. They're usually better able to move on and take responsibility for themselves once other people have stopped pretending that the answers are obvious.

In schools, time is precious and people are always busy. But sometimes it *feels* as if there's no time to listen when the truth is that we're feeling inadequate to the task. Even if there *was* time, even if we *made* time, we worry about being overwhelmed by other people's neediness, by their chaos and desperation. We work in schools because we care passionately about people and want to help them, but on a bad day, when it feels as if we're surrounded by unhappiness, we can end up feeling as if we simply haven't got enough *love* for everyone. 'There isn't enough time!' we complain.

When it comes to love and when it comes to time, we can only do what we can do. It's kinder to be clear about time and important to remember that a little can be a lot.

WHAT IF I'M NOT THE RIGHT PERSON TO HELP?

We may be only too aware of our limitations, having been told during our careers never to think of ourselves as 'counsellors'. We may feel unconfident, unqualified to help someone, having never experienced anything similar in our own lives. And yet still people want to talk to us!

'Why me?'

The unspoken answer will be 'Because I like you!' or 'Because you seem to like me!' or 'Because I think I can trust you!' or 'Because I admire you!' or 'Because I think you might be a bit like me yourself!'

Whatever the reason and however ill-equipped for the task we may feel, it's not fair to run away from someone in need. Sometimes we panic and say, 'Have you thought of talking to someone else?', which can sound as if we're saying 'I can't be bothered to listen!' or 'You're too needy and messed up for my liking!'

However undeserving we may feel, it's us to whom people attach. We may well matter to them more than we think we should, but that's not how the other person sees it. For some people, attaching to anyone is hard. There are people who have been consistently betrayed and let down in their lives; their most important relationships have been disrupted, often from the very beginning of their lives; they've been torn away from the people who could and should have been looking after them. As a result, it's become difficult for them to trust anyone and, understandably, their lives are sometimes dogged by an inability to be close to other people. Their need to be loved has never gone away, but the prospect of loving and being loved by anyone has become very scary.

So for some people who need you to listen, their relationship with you may matter far more to them than it does to you. For them, whether or not you 'say the right thing' and whether or not you consider yourself to be a 'good listener' is irrelevant. Simply having your attention and feeling liked by you will be hugely important, even if they appear not to care.

'I hate this school!'

'Because?'

'Because no one cares!'

'About you?'

'About anyone! No one cares about anyone except themselves!'

'At school? Or at home as well?'

Feelings that we have about people at school will often relate to feelings that we have about far more important people in our lives: the people at home who do or don't, did or didn't care about us. Often it's them that the conversation really needs to be about.

'Home's just as bad as school!'

'So how *are* things at home?'

'A nightmare! How long have you got?'

'Not long. But we've got a few minutes before the bell. How's your mum?'

AS A LISTENER, WHAT EXACTLY AM I TRYING TO ACHIEVE?

We worry that we're expected to work miracles but effective listening is really about one human being trying to understand another. Feeling understood, we feel relieved, better able to bear whatever it is that's going wrong. Feeling understood, our lives seem less daunting. In talking with someone, we may be secretly hoping for miraculous, practical solutions but know perfectly well that – nine times out of ten – there aren't any or we'd have thought of them already. We know that we're in a tough situation, but knowing that someone understands this makes the situation feel more bearable.

The need to be understood is primitive, going back to our experience as babies, desperately needing a parent to understand what it is that we're trying to say. The trouble is that babies have only one word – 'Waaaah!' – to cover a multitude of possibilities. 'Waaaah!' might mean that we're hungry, or wet, or too hot. We hope to attract someone's attention and hope that whoever comes will understand our crying correctly. When that happens, our baby-relief is obvious.

As we get older, most of us get better at bearing the anxiety of not being understood but the underlying *need* to be understood never changes. The youngest child in school will need to feel understood, as will the oldest member of staff or the most seemingly competent parent, because when we're *not* understood, we feel as if we're on our own, different from other people, as if we don't exist. That's a terrifying feeling, which is why some people – young and old – end up screaming so loudly, losing their tempers, refusing to do as they're told, drawing attention to their fear and distress: anything to get people to pay attention and understand.

As listeners, our first job is to understand. We're unlikely to be able to solve another person's problem. Understanding what it feels like for the other person may be as much as we can do, but that will be an end in itself, that will be an achievement.

So what exactly is it that we're trying to understand? Some people will struggle to say anything at all while others will tell long, elaborate stories: this happened, that happened, I said this, he said that... Stories expand to fill the time available and, as a busy professional, you don't have much time, so you need to work out what's important in all that you're being told.

How a person feels will be the most important thing to understand. In many ways, schools are thinking factories where we teach students to think clearly, think often and think for a long time. Yet what always gets in the way of students' thinking is how they're feeling. When they're full of feelings, especially feelings of fear and anxiety, they can't think very well. There are simple neurological reasons for this: the cerebral cortex (the thinking part of the brain) stops working properly when the amygdala (the primitive fear response), responding to the possibility of danger, overwhelms the hippocampus, the part of the brain which helps the cerebral cortex to make sense of what's happening. So until students have calmed down, until they've had a chance to talk about how they're feeling, it's hard for them to think clearly. Adults are the same.

If you pay attention, you can see or hear another person's feelings. They might be obvious in the way that a facial expression changes or in the way that a body suddenly shifts. For example, you ask a boy how he's getting on with his dad. 'Fine!' he says, but saying so, immediately wraps his arms across his chest. Or you see a girl whose face is looking calm while her foot taps impatiently, betraying the fact that she's not calm at all. At other times, you'll hear the feelings in the urgency with which someone tells their story, in the emphases they put on certain things or in remarks that stand out.

'I'm really looking forward to the holidays,' says the girl sitting with you on the playground bench, 'apart from visiting my mum...'

'I was never any good when I was at school,' says the father, worried about his son's progress. 'I don't think I'm going to be of much use to him...'

The feelings might be obvious because a person spends so long telling you something, endlessly going over the same ground, emphasizing the feeling. But this isn't always the case. Sometimes the really important feeling is slipped in as a joke or mentioned only for the talker suddenly to change the subject.

'I'm really starting to hate Mondays,' says your colleague over coffee. 'Anyway, how are you?'

Sometimes the most important feeling gets mentioned right at the end of a conversation, when there's no time left to talk.

'To be honest, I don't know if I can carry on with school much longer,' says the panic-stricken boy whose exams are approaching. 'Oh, is that the bell? Got to go!'

The most important part of understanding another person is trying to understand his or her feelings.

HOW DO I SHOW THAT
I UNDERSTAND?

It may be that we never fully understand what it's like to be someone else. So saying 'I understand' may not always be convincing. People will be able to tell whether or not you really understand without you needing to spell it out: they'll read it in your face, in your body language, in the little things you say, in the kind of questions you ask. Most of the time you might find yourself understanding bits rather than everything.

When you don't understand, it's better to say so. It allows you to be curious, trying to work things out, 'Sorry, can you explain that again? I still don't think I've quite understood.' This shows that you really *do* want to understand and, importantly, that the other person remains the expert on his or her own life – not you. Your role is to be guided towards a better understanding.

People are afraid of being misunderstood but are even more afraid of not being understandable in the first place. So sometimes it helps to summarize what you think you've understood so far: 'Let me see if I've got this right... You and your mum were really close until her boyfriend moved in and now it feels to you like you're being pushed out and like she doesn't care any more?'

'Well, not exactly... I know she cares but we never get any time to talk and she's always taking his side in arguments.'

'Which feels unfair and leaves you feeling really angry with her?'

'Yeah!'

It's okay not to understand as long as you're genuinely trying to understand and not jumping to conclusions.

WHAT IF I CAN'T HELP?

There's an unconscious phenomenon called 'projective identification' whereby people get us to feel their feelings for them. They don't plan this and, because it's unconscious, they don't know that they're doing it, but it's very powerful when it happens. Listening to someone talk, for example, you find yourself feeling more and more helpless (or angry or frustrated) while the person talking appears to be endlessly calm and reasonable. Projective identification is a way of describing wind-ups. When one person can't bear his own feelings, he gets another person to feel them for him. As listeners, we might end up feeling quite helpless when, in fact, helpless is what the person talking is actually feeling but can't acknowledge. So when you're feeling helpless or angry or frustrated, it's always worth wondering whether the feeling is really yours.

As listeners, feeling that we can't help or haven't helped is normal. What matters is remembering that the most important things in life *don't* have obvious solutions or answers. The honest answer to the question, 'Why is my life so hard?' is usually 'You're right, life is hard. Bad things *have* happened to you, things that you haven't deserved. They may not have been anyone's fault but that doesn't mean that they haven't been hard.'

'So what should I do?' asks the parent, rocking the pushchair at the back of the hall as children file out of assembly.

You say that you don't know (because you don't) and ask, 'What do *you* think you should do?'

Surprisingly, a lot of people will come up with possible solutions of their own if you give them back the responsibility. But a few will persist with, 'I don't know! That's why I'm asking you!'

You might offer a selection of possible ideas if you have any but, probably, they'll all be rejected.

'I've tried that. There's nothing I *can* do!'

Sometimes the most useful and truthful thing to say is that there's no answer, no solution. The other person might not thank you for saying this but will be quietly reassured to know that she's not being stupid.

'I'm afraid I don't know what you should do. I think you're in a really difficult situation.'

'I'm glad you've said that! I was worrying in case it was just me! Maybe I'll trying talking to him again...'

As listeners, our priority isn't to fix things but to understand them: we're trying to understand how another person's life feels, how it *really* feels. The feelings that most need our understanding will be the darkest ones because they'll be the ones that no one else will want to hear: feelings of despair, rage, desolation, abandonment, grief, futility. Trying to understand these feelings is always helpful.

And, occasionally, you'll get to hear about someone's happiness and joy!

WHAT IF I GET UPSET MYSELF?

From time to time, the things people talk about will touch you. You might feel sorry for the other person; you might feel angry or sad on their behalf. You might even find yourself crying in sympathy. That doesn't matter. What does matter is that you don't confuse your own experience with the experience of the other person. In the heat of the moment, it's tempting to say, 'I know exactly what you're going through!', to which the heartfelt but unspoken reply will be 'Yes, but you're not me, are you! You *don't* know exactly what I'm going through!'

When we've experienced similar things ourselves, it can actually make listening harder, not easier, because we're more likely to jump to conclusions, more likely to make assumptions about what the other person must be feeling based on our own experience.

Most people want to talk about their everyday concerns – their frustrations, sadnesses and confusions. To be helpful, you don't need to have experienced similar events in your life. What matters is trying to understand how it feels for the other person. Funnily enough, it's sometimes helpful *not* to have experienced the same things if it allows us to be more curious, genuinely trying to understand. The events of another person's life may be quite unfamiliar to you but you'll still be able to understand some of the underlying feelings. For example, you may never have experienced the death of a parent but you'll have experienced loss in your life. You may never have been in a fight but you'll have some idea of what it's like to feel angry or powerless or humiliated.

Occasionally, someone will want to talk about something that sounds scary or momentous. For example, your colleague tells you that he's been having an affair and is going to split up with his wife. Or a student insists that, because she refused to speak to him for five years, she feels responsible for her father's cancer and death. Or a desperate parent confesses to locking her children out of the house for two hours yesterday. **Your job is to hang in there and do your human best, knowing that you can't put parents back together, can't bring loved ones back from the dead and can't stop people being cruel to each other.**

On a school trip, you're sitting with a colleague at the front of the coach, talking about the approaching summer holidays. She goes quiet and you notice that her eyes look tearful. You ask what's up and she tells you that, six months ago, she had an abortion.

She asks, 'Do you think I'm a terrible person?'

Your job as a listener isn't to sit in judgment on other people and so your views on abortion don't matter. What matters is the story that she may be about to tell you and the feelings with which she'll have been living for the past six or more months. Let her tell her story. You may be the first person she's told. Let her describe the conflicts she may have been feeling. Let her cry if she needs to. Listen to her.

Ten minutes later she asks again, 'So, do you think I'm terrible?'

Don't panic and don't pass judgment. Saying yes or no won't change anything for her. In situations like these, we worry about saying the wrong thing and making someone feel worse. Professional counsellors have the same fears. What they do is to meet regularly with someone usually more experienced who they call their 'supervisor', someone who doesn't tell them what to do but who listens and helps them to untangle and make sense of any relationships with which they're struggling. As listeners, our conversations in school may be hugely important but, for the most part, won't be hugely problematic. When they *do* become problematic, though, when you're left feeling particularly useless or upset or scared, it helps to have someone in school to talk with. A school counsellor can be a wonderful resource in these situations but, without an available counsellor, there will be other trusted members of staff who, behind the scenes, can help you to make sense of things. If confidentiality is a problem, you can always talk without mentioning the name of whoever you've been supporting. The point of the conversation is to help you with *your* thinking, not to come up with more solutions on behalf of other people.

Getting help for yourself is often the most professional, responsible way of continuing to help someone else.

AS A LISTENER, WHAT EXACTLY DO I SAY?

Rather than ask lots of questions, encourage the other person to tell you the story. If they can also tell you their feelings as part of that story, then good. If they can't, then as the story unfolds, it's worth trying tentatively to ask about those feelings. Questions like 'What did you feel? What are you feeling? What did it feel like?' may be clichéd but they're the most important questions you can ever ask. 'What did you think?' or 'What are you thinking?' are less important questions because in schools we get regular opportunities to say what we think.

Say less rather than more. In our anxiety to be good listeners, we sometimes feel bound to speak in order to prove that we've been listening and have got worthwhile things to say. But you can say a lot with your facial expressions, with a nod of the head, a raised eyebrow. Sometimes the most useful things to say are little linking conjunctions such as 'And then?' or 'Because?' or simple encouragements such as 'Go on…' or 'What happened next?'

When you do ask questions, ask 'open' rather than 'closed' questions. Closed questions have a one-word answer like 'yes', 'no' or 'maybe'. 'Are you feeling unhappy?' is a closed question with a one-word answer. 'How are you feeling?' is an open question because the person answering has the opportunity to answer in all sorts of ways. Inevitably, you'll need to ask a few closed questions, but if you find yourself asking lots of them, you'll be doing most of the talking and you'll soon be exhausted!

There won't be easy answers. If, at the end of the story, the other person really needs you to say something supportive, then you can say things like, 'That sounds really tough!' or 'I'm not surprised you're angry!' or 'You've certainly been through a lot!' or 'It sounds like it's been really difficult!'

Avoid platitudes like 'I'm sure it'll get better' or 'Time is a great healer' or 'At least there are some positives'. Although well-intentioned, these statements are actually *not* very consoling for someone going through hell. Better to acknowledge what the person is feeling and not offer cheerful optimism. People are more likely to be consoled if they know that they've been genuinely understood.

Talking with you, some people will worry that what they're saying just doesn't make sense. It can help them if you say what you've understood by way of a summary. 'So what you're saying is that he was picking on you and you were feeling trapped…' or 'It sounds like everything's been going wrong lately and that's left you feeling really angry…' or 'What I've understood is that this has been going on for ages and it feels to you like someone should have been doing something about it… Is that right?'

WHAT IF I DON'T KNOW WHAT TO SAY?

Effective listening is about saying less rather than more. So if you don't know what to say, say nothing. Saying nothing gives you time to think. The danger is that we get anxious when we don't know what to say and end up blurting out any old thing to make ourselves feel better. Try to keep quiet. (You can look thoughtfully at the floor or ceiling if necessary!) If you wait and say nothing, the other person will often interrupt the silence, continuing the story. Sometimes the most honest thing to say is 'I don't know what to say!' Surprisingly, lots of people will find this helpful and will be only too happy to carry on talking.

For some people, silence is uncomfortable, and these people will undoubtedly need you to say things, but, for other people, silence is a luxury, a chance to let thoughts and feelings emerge and settle without interruption. Your job is to decide what kind of response the other person needs from you. Problems arise when the listener no longer trusts that listening and trying to understand are enough and – panicking – starts to think that she should be coming up with practical solutions to the other person's problems, trying to make everything better.

It takes confidence to acknowledge that we don't know the answers, that we haven't got solutions. But it's true, and it's oddly reassuring for people who are complaining that they don't know what to think or do. It means that they're not silly, not missing a trick. It means that they're not stupid. When it comes to so many of life's difficulties, most of us *don't* know what to think or do. In fact, not knowing is how we spend most of our lives! 'Am I loved? Is he really right for me? Am I making the most of my life?

Should I get a job in another school? Am I a good enough parent? Am I being a good friend?' Often, our panic comes from feeling that we *should* have the answers to these questions. So we talk and talk, worrying all the while about not having the answers. When the person in whom we're confiding – the listener – doesn't know either, it's actually a relief! It reminds us that we have to take responsibility for our own lives: no one's going to do it for us.

'So you're saying that you don't know what I should do?'

'Yes, I think you're in a really difficult situation.'

'But I thought you'd be able to help me with it!'

'I can suggest things but I won't be suggesting anything that you haven't already thought of yourself. It's hard to know what to do in situations like these.'

'Okay, but just tell me what you think. Do you think I should I stay with him or leave him?'

'Tell me what *you* think...'

WHAT IF SOMEONE ASKS FOR ADVICE?

Effective listening means trying to understand, not jumping in with lots of advice. The trouble is that not many people will approach you and ask to be understood. That would sound weird! So they'll ask for advice because asking for advice sounds vaguely grown up and doesn't betray any desperation. 'I need your advice,' they'll say. 'You'll never guess what's happened!' What they mean is that they need to tell you their story, hoping that you'll understand, and understand especially what they're feeling. They're *not* actually asking for advice. They know perfectly well that a good listener can't stop unfairnesses from happening. And they probably know what to do as well: that's the easy bit. The hard bit is doing it and living with all the feelings, memories and relationships. That's the bit they need to talk about.

SHOULD I TALK ABOUT MY OWN EXPERIENCES?

There are some listeners who make a point of never sharing their own experiences. In schools, this can seem weird and can be quite unsettling for the other person. Good listening is about making the conversation seem as normal as possible, and in normal conversations there's give and take. Yet, at the same time, the point of good listening is to listen and not talk too much. It's never helpful when the listener embarks on a story which effectively trumps the other person's, as if to say, 'Huh! You think your life's hard! You should hear what happened to me!'

Sometimes it might help if you, as the listener, share an experience of your own, but before doing so you should ask yourself why you're doing it. 'Am I about to share this because I genuinely think it'll help the other person or is it because I can't hold on to it any longer? Is it because I'm moved and I've got to get it off my chest? Is it because sharing this will make the other person like me more? Who's this going to be for, really?' **It can be very tempting to share your own experience, but be scrupulous with yourself. If it's really for the other person and what the other person most needs from you right now, then maybe. But if it's really to make yourself feel better, don't do it.**

Needless to say, your failures will be of more interest to other people than your successes.

IS IT OKAY TO HUG A PERSON?

There's no rule about this but the same dilemma applies... 'Who's the hug for? Am I putting my arm around her shoulder because that's what she most needs me to do or am I doing it because I'm desperate to show how much I sympathize?' Sometimes we hug people to reassure ourselves when we're anxious or don't know what to say. Of course hugs can sometimes feel supportive but, at other times, they can feel too much. We can end up smothering the other person with intended kindness. A hug also can stop a person from talking. If someone's crying, that's fine: he may be crying because he can, not because he's weak or failing. Crying is normal and a crying person doesn't necessarily need hugging. He might just need time to cry without anyone interrupting or making a big deal out of it.

It's usually better to support a person with words rather than hugs.

WHAT IF I DON'T LIKE SOMEONE?

The old distinction between liking the person but disliking the behaviour is important. Of course we always try to like the person even when we can't stand the behaviour. We might disapprove of what she does or says, but once we dig down into the feelings informing her behaviour, we find another human being like ourselves, full of vulnerabilities, hopes and fears, capable of cruelty as well as kindness.

There's a process called 'projection' that happens unconsciously in relationships whereby we can't help but see ourselves reflected in other people. We project on to them the parts of ourselves about which we feel uncomfortable, seeing our bad selves reflected in them. So, for example, if we know that we're inclined to be two-faced and don't like that about ourselves, we project it onto someone else, saying, 'I don't like him! He's so two-faced!' We keep away from people who remind us of these unlikable parts of ourselves, and we're drawn to people on to whom we project the likeable parts of ourselves. 'I really like you because you're so honest' might translate as 'I like the fact that *I'm* so honest!'

When you find a person hard to like, it's worth wondering whether that's because he or she reminds you of parts of yourself that you'd rather not be reminded of... your cowardice, for example, or your deceitfulness, bossiness, laziness, your tendency to complain – the list might be endless! If you can be honest with yourself about this, then you can be clearer about whether the other person is actually as unpleasant as she seems.

WHAT IF THEY GET ANGRY WITH ME?

If someone does get angry with you, it might be frightening but probably won't be as personal as it feels. 'Transference' is another unconscious process that happens between people. In short, we're born into some kind of family. These first family relationships leave a decisive imprint on us so that, later in our lives, we tend to 'transfer' on to people in the present feelings that we have about these people from the past. Indeed, we start behaving towards people in the present *as if they were* the people from the past.

Teachers get this all the time. Because they can't help but be parent-figures (occasionally even getting called 'Mum' or 'Dad'), they remind people of their actual parents and get treated as if they were. So the reason why I think that one teacher is wonderful might have nothing whatsoever to do with her ability as a teacher and everything to do with the fact that she reminds me (unconsciously) of my wonderful mum. Or I might loathe another teacher because he reminds me (unconsciously) of my dreadful dad. I might like one teacher because she's The Mum I Always Wanted while despising another teacher for being completely *unlike* my fantastic dad.

These unconscious transferences go on in relationships all the time. And there are sibling transferences. A lot of the befriending or squabbling behaviour in classrooms and playgrounds stems from the (unconscious) feelings that we have about our siblings. When we feel jealous of our siblings, we tend to feel jealous of our classmates.

All sorts of transferential feelings are heaped upon the poor headteacher. He or she can't help but represent the mother or father with whom we've always fought or from whom we've always sought approval. Adults joke about their fear of 'going into the headteacher's office' but that's never just a joke about schooldays: it's also a statement about the power of what the headteacher represents.

For transferential reasons, people sometimes get very angry with us when we haven't done anything to deserve it.

'This school's done nothing for my daughter!' says the parent, leaning forward angrily, glaring at the headteacher.

The headteacher explains all the practical things that have been done to ensure that Mrs. Clarke's five-year-old daughter isn't getting bullied. In fact, he's spent a lot of the last fortnight putting into place people and systems to ensure that Alice is safe. 'So I'm sorry that you're feeling this way,' he says.

Mrs. Clarke is having none of it. 'Alice feels that no one cares about her at this school!' she says. 'None of your teachers ever ask how she's feeling, and she says that you yourself saw her sitting in assembly yesterday and didn't even speak to her!'

By now it's clear to the headteacher that he can't win because there's a complete mismatch between Mrs. Clarke's perception and any objective reality. Perhaps Mrs. Clarke felt bullied herself when she was at school. It'll almost certainly be the case that she feels like this in her life at the moment: uncared for, unnoticed and unimportant. And all of this gets blamed on the headteacher as the parent-figure still allegedly failing Mrs. Clarke after all these years.

Sometimes we can be doing a good job as listeners and yet still people get angry with us. Usually it's not our fault but is probably because we're unwittingly reminding them of the person with whom they really are angry! Pointing this out at the time may not always be helpful (rather the opposite!), but knowing that it's not as personal as it feels helps us to weather the storm.

WHAT IF SOMEONE DOESN'T WANT TO TALK?

You can't make people talk. Some people are quite unused to talking about themselves; other people simply don't have words for certain feelings. Most people need the listener to hang in there, enduring the awkward silences and staying patient as – slowly – they try to talk.

'How are things?'

'Fine!'

'Fine…?'

'Yeah, nothing interesting.'

'Apart from the usual?'

'Yeah, the usual crap!'

'Like parents? Like school?'

'Yeah, all of that!'

'Go on...'

Some people find it hard to believe that anyone's prepared to listen because, in their experience, no one *has* ever listened or been interested. They don't want to talk because they simply don't trust the situation. It's too weird. They prefer to be getting on with something practical and then sometimes they can talk a little as they go along.

Some people don't want to talk because they're afraid of what might come out. They're afraid that they might start crying and never stop or that they might get angry and scare someone. They might offer tantalizing scraps. Alluding to the situation at home, for example, a parent might mutter, 'You wouldn't want to know!' Or at the end of the day, a colleague might say goodbye, adding that he's off to 'another evening of misery!' A student might look away from you, saying that she's okay, 'But not really!'

Your first job is to respect the other person's right to say nothing. It may be that he or she has said enough for now and will talk again on another occasion. You can't force the pace. **Your second job is to imagine what the other person would say if only she could...** What might she be feeling? What might she be thinking but *not* saying? What might she be needing from you? This is where your intuition and empathy are important. But intuition and empathy can be quite wrong, so don't jump to conclusions!

In situations like these, it sometimes helps to wonder aloud. 'I wonder what it felt like for you... I wonder what you're thinking... I wonder about the things that are hard for you to say...' 'I wonder' is a very useful way of starting a sentence because it's not a question. Because of that, the other person doesn't feel obliged to answer and doesn't have to worry about getting the answer wrong.

'I wonder how things are for you at home…'

No answer.

'I wonder if they've got harder…'

'No, easier! My dad left!'

It doesn't matter if what you're wondering is wrong because the other person will often leap into the conversation to correct you. 'I wonder' also allows you to float thoughts which might be helpful for the other person to think about once you've parted. 'I wonder' can stir things. But gently, without force.

And sometimes 'I wonder' makes no difference at all! Sometimes the conversation needs to end because the other person has said all he can say for now. A little can be a lot. Rather than persist, it's better to leave things open so that he can come back and talk some more in the future without feeling pressurized.

'You've mentioned some really important things. I'd be keen to hear more in the future, but I'll leave that up to you. Stop me in school and let me know when you'd like to talk some more…'

As busy professionals we offer students, colleagues and parents what little time we have. We don't have time to play games, chasing after people who would rather not talk. But on the other hand, we do have to be patient and vigilant, remembering that – much as they may *want* to talk – it's genuinely hard for some people to do so. That's frustrating for us, of course, but even more frustrating for them.

WHAT IF THEY CAN'T SAY WHAT THEY FEEL?

It's rare to feel a single, simple emotion. We might feel the pain of someone's death, for example, whilst at the same time feeling a strong sense of relief. We might feel angry whilst also feeling hurt. We might feel powerful whilst also feeling afraid. Often the things we feel seem contradictory. We might love *and* hate a parent; we might want to go and stay; we might long to grow up and yet remain a child. However contradictory they may seem, both feelings are likely to be true. In these situations we might accurately describe ourselves as feeling ambivalent – having mixed feelings – but we're more likely to say that we don't know what we're feeling.

'How are you feeling?'

'Don't know.'

'Happy? Sad?'

'Don't know.'

The theory goes that a baby is born experiencing its mother as wholly good. But very quickly it realizes that there are times when she doesn't understand, when she's distracted and irritable. The baby concludes that it must have two mothers: a good, satisfying one and a bad, unsatisfying one. This makes simple sense to a tiny baby but, as it grows up, the baby has to learn that these two mothers are one and the same person, a mixture of good and bad qualities. Accepting this takes most of us a lifetime and, in the meantime, when things go wrong, when the pressure's on, we easily revert to the old idea of a good mother and a bad mother, a good school and a bad school, a world that loves us and a world that hates us.

Being able to acknowledge a mix of feelings is progress for most of us. **When someone says that he doesn't know**

what he feels, it usually means that he's feeling mixed.
But people who feel mixed often worry that they're not
making sense, that they should be feeling one thing and
one thing alone:

'I hate this school!'
'Hate it?'
'Yeah!'
'Because you had such hopes for it?'
'No, I just hate it.'
'Hate being disappointed by it?'
'Yeah!'
'It's hard when it's not the way we want it to be.'
'It's not just hard, it's bloody annoying!'
'Annoying and disappointing?'
'Yeah!'
'Hurtful as well?'

Saying 'I don't know!' can be a way of avoiding
difficult questions, but it's also true that sometimes we
don't **know things: we don't know what to feel, what**
to think, who to trust, what to hope for... And the
process of 'knowing' can't be speeded up. Young people,
in particular, feel better when we acknowledge that their 'I
don't know!' may well be the truth and that, when it comes
to feelings and relationships, not knowing is a perfectly
honorable, understandable position.

WHAT ABOUT CONFIDENTIALITY?

You can't promise complete confidentiality to anyone
because you don't know what you're about to hear. It's
always best to be explicit about where you stand: yes, most
things you'll be able to keep to yourself, but if a child or

young person is in danger or is being hurt then you'll need to tell someone about that. Usually it helps to give examples. This is what all the other professionals in school are also saying about confidentiality so it's unlikely to be a surprise, at least to students.

'Can I talk to you, Miss?'

'Of course you can.'

'Will you tell anyone?'

'That depends. If someone's in danger or is being hurt, then it wouldn't be fair to keep that a secret. But I don't need to tell anyone about all the other things.'

'Are you sure?'

'Quite sure.'

'Oh dear! I don't know whether to say. I don't know if you'll have to tell someone.'

'Well, tell me what's happened and then we can decide the best thing to do.'

'I'm not sure… The thing is, I think my hamster's died.'

Colleagues will also need to know whether you'll keep it secret if they tell you things. Again, it's important not to promise absolute confidentiality. A colleague may be potentially endangering other people by drinking or taking drugs before school, or he may simply be unfit to come to school in the first place because of an illness or because of things that are going on in his life.

Sometimes we worry that passing on information in these situations will mean that no one confides in us again. But people confide in us for a reason. They're *more* likely to tell us things knowing that we'll act, than if we promise to keep everything hush-hush. Often people will talk to us after thinking about it for months, weighing up the consequences, picking the right moment.

The same goes for parents when they talk to us in the playground or at official meetings or when we meet them, by chance, in the supermarket. Again, you have to be clear. If children or young people are at risk, you'll act. If adults are at risk, you may not be obliged to act but may nevertheless feel that, as a good citizen, you can't turn a blind eye when you hear about domestic violence, for example, or about other crimes which put people in danger.

Having said that, schools are full of gossip. So when people confide in us and there's no risk to anyone (as is usually the case), it's vital that we *do* respect the other person's confidentiality and *don't* tell other people. That might mean agreeing with the other person how you'll behave when you next bump into each other with other people around.

'When I see you around, I'll say hello as usual. But I won't ask you about the things that we've just been talking about. Not because I'm not interested and wondering, but because it wouldn't be fair to start that conversation with other people around and when we're both in the middle of doing other things. Instead, we'll save it for the next time we talk properly.'

WHAT IF SOMEONE JUST WANTS ATTENTION?

Everyone wants attention. There's nothing shameful or abnormal about that. Babies have to get their parents' attention in order to survive and that need for attention never goes away. Most of us are lucky in that we can take the attention of other people for granted. But not everyone can do that. For some people, it's terrifying not to have other people's attention.

Needing attention means needing attachment. Until we feel safely attached, we feel anxious and are likely to panic when things go wrong. A lot of disruptive behaviour in school is really an inarticulate plea for attention, for relationships that last. **Needing attention also means needing to be interesting.** A baby has to interest its parents to survive. That's why we all dread being boring because we imagine that – as boring people – we'll be overlooked and taken for granted. But when other people find us interesting, we relax. In order to be interesting, some people tell exaggerated or made-up stories about themselves because they don't believe that telling the truth will be sufficiently interesting to another person.

'My mum might have cancer! And my dad's probably got to go to court because of something he never did! And one of my brothers was going to be a speedway rider but they think he might have broken his leg!'

'That sounds really bad. But before we talk about those things, how are you? What have you been up to?'

Babies desperately need attention and need to be interesting, but they also have to learn to share their parents with other people. By extension, the people needing our attention in school must also learn that they can't have us all to themselves; that we have other people to see, other things to do during the day. So rather than trail around distractedly with someone constantly following and trying to interrupt you, it's better to give that person a fixed amount of your full attention. And then move on. With a child, that might mean giving him an allocated, guaranteed amount of time each day: three minutes perhaps in which to tell you everything…

'…and then I'm going to get on with seeing the other people.'

'But can I talk to you again later?'

'No. We've got our time together now and no one's going to take it away from you. And when our time's up, I'm going to be seeing other people.'

'But what if I get upset?'

'Then you're going to find someone else to talk with, or, better still, you'll wait until tomorrow when we have our next time together.'

There's nothing childish about needing attention. As professionals, we've learned to wait our turn. But we still know what it's like to feel overlooked and taken for granted. And we know how we feel like reacting on these occasions. It's helpful to acknowledge our own need if that helps us to understand and tolerate other people's need for attention.

WHAT IF THEY'RE REALLY CLINGY?

We attach in order to feel safe and ultimately to survive because, in evolutionary terms, we can't survive alone. So our need to attach is primitive. We don't make a choice about it. When we're afraid, we cling to whatever we imagine will keep us safe. The people we call 'clingy' in school may seem young for their age because they are. A fifteen-year-old may be acting like a five-year-old because there's a part of him that still *is* a five-year-old, still needing what that five-year-old never got or never got enough of: recognition, love, a sense of mattering, a feeling of safety.

'Sir, can I talk to you? I *really* need to talk to you!'

However inconvenient it may be, it's important not to punish people for making attachments to us. For them, trusting anyone enough to make an attachment may be progress and they'll only be able to move on

once they've had enough of whatever it is that they're needing. If they can't attach to us, they might attach instead to someone unsuitable, or might attach to some kind of behaviour – to cutting or starving themselves, for example, or to drinking and using illegal drugs…

In an ideal world, it sometimes helps to give clingy people *more* time rather than less but, inevitably, that time will always need to be boundaried. Once people know that they'll get their share of your time, they relax, knowing that they won't be forgotten and that you won't break your promise. Once they know that you'll stick to your time boundary, they relax further, knowing that pushing for more time is futile.

'I'm afraid our time's up.'

'But, Sir, there are still loads of things I haven't told you about!'

'Good, because I'll look forward to hearing about those things next time.'

'But we've only had a few minutes!'

'I know, and I've appreciated hearing about everything. It's always a shame when we have to finish but I'll look forward to seeing you next time!'

3

HELPING PEOPLE...

WHO ARE STRUGGLING WITH FAMILY RELATIONSHIPS

If they trust you enough and if you've got enough time, people will almost always end up talking about their families, because that's where everything starts.

We may complain and speculate in the staffroom about 'school', but the reason we feel so strongly about this thing called 'school' is because 'school' is often an unconscious reminder of how we feel about our families. That's why students get so angry about school; that's why parents are often so critical and why colleagues get so wound up... School is run by a collection of parent-figures and, ultimately, by one parent-figure – the headteacher. In school, we're endlessly comparing ourselves with other people, assessing our own importance, wondering whether we're valued, noticed, liked. 'School' provokes strong feelings about being looked after or not looked after. So how we behave in school usually reflects how we feel about home. This is most obviously true for children and young people who will often take out on 'school' their feelings about home. We do our best to curb their misbehaviour with incentives and threats but, in their heads, most students know perfectly well how to behave: the trouble is that their feelings get the better of them.

Sometimes the only thing that makes a difference is listening to these feelings and, usually, that means listening to the stories about a person's life at home and all the feelings about home fuelling that person's behaviour in school.

'How are things out of school?' isn't an intrusive question. You're not forcing anyone to say anything. A few people will simply answer, 'Fine!' and change the subject, but most will seize the opportunity to talk about things at home. Some might look at you doubtfully and joke, 'How long have you got?' But 'How long have you got?' is a serious question. If they're going to answer your question about things out of school, they don't want to be cut off in mid-story because you've suddenly got to go. They need you to be clear about time.

'How long have you got?'

'Six minutes.'

In those six minutes you might be told anything. You'll almost certainly be told about parents. You might hear about step-parents, new partners and babies, half-siblings, grandparents... You'll hear about how things have changed over the years, about broken promises, betrayals, bad behaviour, sudden events and a thousand domestic unfairnesses.

Forget the advice: your job is to listen, and listen especially for the strongest feelings. You're following the emotional smoke. People will feel better for having told you their anger or hatred, sadness or frustration. Having told you about how they're feeling at home, they'll be less likely to enact their feelings in school at other people's expense. And if they need to talk for longer, be clear about whether or not that's going to be possible.

'My mum's doing my head in!'

'How come?'

'Just the way she is! She's always having a go at me when I haven't done anything. She's on at me the whole time! I'll be in my bedroom trying to do my homework and she'll come in and find something to have a go at me about. And if I have a go at her, she'll ground me or take away my phone!'

'Like you can't ever win?'

'Exactly! And it's *so* annoying! She lets my brother do anything! If he's late in, he never gets told off! If there's dishes to do, he never has to do them! It's always me!'

'And then you come to school in the morning and have to act like everything's okay...'

'Yeah, and that's not easy, especially when the teachers are always having a go at me as well!'

'I wonder what you feel like saying to all these people?'

'I feel like saying... Can I swear?'

WHO NEED TO TALK ABOUT DEATH

We get scared of death and scared of talking about death. We worry about upsetting other people or making things worse for them.

Sometimes when someone's dying or has just died, there's a conspiracy of silence and no one will talk about it. This is usually unhelpful. **While no one should ever**

be forced to talk about death (or anything else), the opportunity to talk should always be there to talk with someone who isn't scared, who won't run away or change the subject, who won't offer false promises and won't try to make everyone look on the bright side. Because the fact is that people do die. It's normal. It's usually upsetting, and that's normal too. Sometimes people die in accidents or die young, which is especially shocking for everyone.

When these things happen, it's a relief to find someone prepared to listen. In schools we're more likely to talk to someone we already know, provided that he or she isn't going to panic, rather than to an outsider, wheeled in especially for the occasion. We don't care whether the person has qualifications in bereavement counselling, we just want to talk with someone we like and who likes us.

And we don't want advice or solutions. We want to be allowed to rant or weep or be angry or tell bad jokes. It'll be our own way of responding to the situation. There isn't a right way. Bereaved people worry that they should be coping better or crying more or crying less. It's important for them to know that you don't mind whether they're talking a lot or talking a little. As ever, the most important thing is trying to understand how the other person is feeling. And, as ever, time spent doing this has to be boundaried because school has to go on, however difficult the situation may be.

WHO ARE STUBBORN

Some people have to be stubborn in order to survive. Their stubbornness is what keeps them safe and stops them getting bossed about. As long as they stay stubborn, no one can make them do anything. 'You can't make me talk!' is absolutely true and very reassuring for a frightened person to be able to say.

Stubbornness is what psychotherapists call a 'defence'. **We all have defences and we need them. They keep us safe. They protect us from humiliation, danger, uncertainty, powerlessness.** We develop them over a lifetime. Sometimes we discard them when the danger has passed, but there are some defences that we stick with all our lives, still using the old behaviours we learned as children – turning everything into a joke, changing the subject, storming out of the room, disrupting other people... Drinking and taking drugs might be defences. Anger might be a defence if it hides what someone's really feeling. Violence might be a defence for someone feeling trapped or powerless or afraid.

You might be sitting with colleagues in the staffroom, listening to the headteacher. Everyone looks attentive and serious, wearing their public faces but, inside, they might be thinking something quite different, 'I wish she'd shut up... God, this is so boring I can't wait to get home... I wish I didn't have to cook this evening!' Your colleagues have learned a way of behaving that's appropriate and necessary in a meeting. They've learned to hide their feelings. They've developed appropriate defences.

Our defences only become a problem if we feel stuck with them, responding in our old defensive ways when we'd like to be responding differently. Stubbornness might still be completely necessary for one person while, for another person, it might have become a curse, stopping that person from ever getting close to other people.

So what helps? Behind every defence is an anxiety of one sort or another. The skill of the listener is in anticipating or second-guessing what that anxiety might be. Why does this child always retreat into anger? Is it because he's afraid of embarrassment or failure? Why does this young person behave so stubbornly when there's no need? Is it because she's afraid of losing control, of feeling powerless? Why does this parent always behave as if a catastrophe is about to happen? Is it because she knows of no other way of getting attention? And why is my colleague always so negative about everything? Is it because he's afraid to hope for good things in case he's disappointed? Or is it for fear of not living up to other people's expectations?

There's always a reason for the defence, and our job as listeners is to puzzle it out because then we won't take the defence at face value. Then we'll realize that there's more to the story than meets the eye and we'll find some way of asking about what's really going on.

'People who don't know you probably just see you as this quiet guy who doesn't say much.'

'Yeah…'

'They wouldn't realize that you're quiet for a reason, not because you haven't got things to say.'

'Yeah…'

'I wonder what you'd say to them if you decided to tell them what you *really* think?'

When people begin to talk about their underlying feelings and anxieties, their presenting behaviour begins to change because that way of behaving, that defence is no longer needed. Talked about, anxieties become less shameful, less powerful, and the need to defend against them is reduced.

You're talking with a student in your tutor group. He's been getting into lots of trouble recently, refusing to do as he's told.

'If people knew you better and could see past your stubbornness,' you say to him, 'I wonder what they'd realize?'

'Dunno!'

'That your stubbornness stops people getting at you? That stuff's happened to you in the past and you're never going to let it happen again?'

'Yeah, maybe... So?'

'So that makes sense,' you continue. 'It stands to reason that when you've been hurt or let down or betrayed or picked on, you're not going to let people do that to you again.'

'Suppose.'

'I wonder what did happen? I wonder if people have always let you down or if stuff happened when you were younger and certain people betrayed you?'

WHO TALK OF SUICIDE

It's a word that frightens most of us, but our fear won't help someone who's feeling suicidal and wanting to talk.

If someone is actively planning their own death, don't keep that to yourself. However good a friend and however supportive a listener you may be, if someone's determined to kill themselves tell someone in authority at school or, with the help of others, find a way of alerting the person's doctor. It's best to do this with permission, but if a suicidal person won't give their permission, do it anyway.

Having said that, people sometimes describe themselves as 'suicidal' when they're feeling very low or when they're *curious* about suicide, wondering what dying would be like and whether they'd be missed: they're not necessarily planning anything. So it's important not to over-react to the word 'suicide' but to do your best to understand the other person's misery. **You can't actually stop anyone – young**

or old – from killing themselves if they're determined enough, but you can try to understand how they're feeling, which often reduces their feelings of isolation.

WHO LACK SELF-ESTEEM

Overcoming challenges and getting praise from other people helps us to feel better about ourselves. But only for a while. Our underlying sense of 'self-esteem' is more primitive, arising from a basic sense of self: 'Who am I? Am I loved? What am I worth?' Lots of people, including professionals in schools, appear very self-assured on the surface, but get them on their own and they'll admit to feeling very differently underneath. So having a robust, confident sense of self is dependent on something more fundamental than winning a race or getting promoted or deserving a round of applause. There's no harm in telling a person with 'low self-esteem' all the things you like about them and no harm in reminding them of their talents. The trouble is that this only goes so far and, for many people, it changes nothing: still they feel worthless or invisible or useless.

We start developing (or not developing) a sense of self from the moment of our birth. At first we can't distinguish between ourselves and other people but, little by little, we begin to do so and we do it by looking in the mirror. But a baby can't jump out of its cot and look at itself in the mirror! Instead, the mirror that a baby looks into is the mirror of the other person's face looking down, reflecting back the baby's facial expressions and sounds. (As adults, we instinctively find ourselves doing this whenever we hold or look at babies.)

This is how a baby begins to develop a sense of itself. But for this to happen, the mirror-face must be there in the first place (not absent or distracted) and must be interested in the baby, attuned to its movements and sounds (not resentful of the baby or depressed). Little by little, the baby and the mirror-face begin to play together, mostly copying each other but sometimes coming up with new and different communications as the baby starts to develop a wider repertoire of how and who it can be. Unfortunately, some babies will develop only a narrow repertoire, a narrow sense of self, because the mirror-face will only reflect back certain things: anger, for example, or fear. Other babies will be worse off still: searching desperately for a mirror – any mirror – to confirm that they even exist in the first place.

Lucky babies will get enough attuned mirroring and will soon start to 'internalize' their mirror – no longer needing the other face to be physically present to confirm their existence because they're starting to take that for granted. Lucky babies will soon be learning to reflect *on themselves*. Unlucky babies, however, won't be able to relax. They'll scream for the mirror-face to come and reassure them. They'll do anything to get its most basic attention because, without it, it's as if they don't exist, and that's terrifying.

Helping someone with 'low self-esteem' means becoming a mirror-face: reflecting them back to themselves, being interested in them, trying to understand them. It's why the simple drip-feed of saying hello to people in school every day and remembering their names is so important: it *recognizes* them. A baby must be recognized by its parent in order to survive – simple as that. Because of this, our fear of *not* being recognized is, at times, overwhelming. We'll do anything to get the recognition, the attention, the mirroring that we need. When we get it, we feel better.

When we get it a lot, we feel good. When we get it all the time, we feel great.

Self-esteem comes from feeling understandable to another person.

WHO ARE ANGRY

It's useful to remind people that the reason why they're angry isn't because there's anything wrong with them but is because they care. If they didn't care, they wouldn't bother getting so angry. Angry people are passionate, not depressed. They believe in fairness. They usually have reason to be angry.

Anger is a healthy emotion. How it's expressed is another matter altogether but, in schools, anger tends to be expressed as swearing or violence, for example, when it can't be expressed as words, either because the angry person has no vocabulary for anger or because no one's prepared to listen to the angry words.

It's also worth remembering that anger is sometimes the *only* feeling that some people are able to express, therefore they do it all the time. In fact, their anger may be covering up a range of subtler emotions that they're feeling but can't express – hurt, emptiness, loneliness and fear, for example. At times, it'll be important not to take someone's anger at face value.

It's also important to remember that anger can't easily be rationalized away. We recommend 'anger management' courses to people in the belief that this will somehow bring their anger under control. But we all need our anger. It gives us our determination. It gets things done. It protects us. The only way we can learn to regulate or 'manage' anger (expressing it appropriately rather than inappropriately) is by having it heard. Babies learn to bear their feelings only because someone spends time bearing those feelings with them until, as they get older, the babies turn into children and into young people having learned to bear the feelings themselves. Psychotherapists would say that they've 'internalized' their relationship with their listener: now they can listen to themselves; they can continue to think while feeling strongly; they can go around behaving appropriately while still fuming inside. Of course, not everyone can do this because not everyone has had enough early experience of being listened to. In schools, we find ourselves listening regularly to the anger of people who haven't been listened to before. This can take time. There are usually no rational or behavioural short-cuts when it comes to anger. And it's worth remembering that good listening is never about trying merely to placate another person but about engaging with that person's strongest feelings. Sometimes this is referred to as 'active' listening: not keeping the other person at a cool, comfortable distance but getting your emotional hands dirty!

'How are things?'

'Terrible!'

'Tell me!'

An easy mistake is to ask angry people lots of 'Why?' questions: 'Why are you angry? Why did you do it? Why can't you apologize?', but when they're full of fury, angry people can't think straight. Fear floods the brain and the hippocampus is temporarily unable to communicate with the cerebral cortex. As a result, questions beginning with 'Why?' which require a thinking answer are precisely the ones that an angry person will find hardest to answer. For this reason we sensibly give angry people opportunities to calm down, 'time out' before expecting them to think clearly again. More useful questions might begin with you saying 'Tell me what happened...' or 'How are you feeling?' Questions about *why* it happened and *why* the person is feeling angry can wait till later.

Listening to other people's anger is made more difficult when no one's listening to our own. We can end up resenting the other person's anger or being scared of it because we're working so hard to subdue our own. We can find ourselves taking revenge on the people who haven't listened to us. In schools, there's anger everywhere. Sometimes it's appropriate, ethical anger at the unfairness of the world; sometimes it's anger at the inadequacy of what a school can provide, expected to solve so many of society's problems; sometimes it's the anger of people who care passionately and therefore get passionately angry.

As professionals, we can't afford to be scared of anyone's anger. We need to find opportunities – a few minutes here and there – to listen to anger expressed as *words*:

'You look really angry...'

'I am!'

'What's happened?'

'They were having a go at me, saying things about my family!'

'In that case, I'm not surprised you're angry.'

'Yeah!'

'Angry and? What else are you feeling?'

'Like hitting someone!'

'If you could hit them with words, what words would you use?'

WHO ARE BEING BULLIED

Wherever there are people, there's the potential for bullying, and so in every school there will, from time to time, be bullying. Bullying behaviour in the staffroom will be subtler but will be just as hurtful and vicious in its way as the bullying in the boys' toilets. Indeed, the bullying in the toilets might reflect the bullying in the staffroom in as much as children will tend to copy the behaviour of their parent-figures.

Children and young people, members of staff and parents will all talk of feeling bullied from time to time. Even the so-called 'bullies' are likely to say that they're feeling bullied! Listening to all these people, it's easy to start feeling helpless – precisely the feeling that the bullied person will be feeling. It's easy to find ourselves snatching at solutions, to which the bullied person will reply, 'I've tried that and it didn't work!' We get more and more indignant on the bullied person's behalf who looks up meekly and says, 'I know, and there's nothing I can do!' Listening to this, we're likely to end up feeling more and more angry, more and more overwhelmed.

With bullying, there's an absolute need for practical action. Someone in school must do something. That might mean intervening to threaten the bullying person with punishment; it might mean following this through and enforcing the punishment. It's unglamorous work but being bullied is horrible and can affect a person for life. So if children and young people are being bullied, you may be the person who has to investigate, has to do the punishing and has to do it quickly to stop the bullying from continuing.

But as a listener, your other job is to listen, despite being made to feel helpless. **If you can bear their feelings of helplessness, it often frees bullied people to act for themselves** because, with bullying, it's easy to get stuck. The person doing the actual bullying may have all sorts of fine qualities but will have got stuck, able only to be nasty. And the person feeling bullied may have all sorts of assertive, creative qualities but will also have got stuck, unable to express those qualities.

Part of our job as listeners is to be interested in those qualities. However much a bullied person may insist that helplessness and hurt are all there is to know, we have to keep a broader perspective. That doesn't mean offering clumsy exhortations like 'Oh come on! I know you can be really determined when you put your mind to it!' It means being interested in all aspects of a person's life. Your message is that feeling bullied is only *one* of the many interesting things about that person. You're also interested in him as a person who plays computer games, goes skateboarding, likes Maths, spends time with his half-sister, believes in animal rights... You're not necessarily trying to cheer him up but trying to recognize and revive the many other roles he also plays. He isn't just 'the bullied boy'.

It's worth remembering that feeling bullied by people in school (or bullied by school) may not be a person's only experience of bullying. Sometimes people have histories of bullying which go back to when they were small, when they first lost confidence or had it taken away from them. Given time, it'll be important to hear about these earlier experiences, especially experiences from family life, which are often the ones that scar us most. Sometimes it's cathartic and empowering to say what we *felt* like saying, but didn't and couldn't say all those years ago.

'I know it's a long time ago and you were only four, but I wonder what you *would* have said if you'd been older and more confident?'

WHO SAY THEY'RE DEPRESSED

It's a word that we use a lot when we mean that we're feeling miserable, sad, disillusioned or fed up. Real, 'clinical' depression is a particularly horrible illness caused either by chemical imbalances occurring naturally in the brain or by events in our lives (especially losses and other big changes) which trigger those imbalances. Clinical depression has physical symptoms such as sleeplessness, loss of energy and appetite. Someone who's clinically depressed will probably struggle to get out of bed and go to school in the morning. In fact, they'll struggle to do most things. Their best course of action will be to visit the doctor, where the treatment for depression will either be drugs to redress the chemical imbalances or counselling and psychotherapy to talk about the losses and changes. Or a combination of drugs and talking.

When things go wrong in our lives and we feel awful, it's easy to conclude that something must be wrong with us, that we must have an illness because we're not normally like this. Yet feeling that life is pointless might be a perfectly sensible response to the death of someone we've loved; feeling furious might be a completely appropriate response to many of the unfairnesses of life; crying night and day might make complete sense when a lover has left us. **Depression and other mental illnesses are real but, at the same time, we have to remind people that normal life *does* sometimes hit us with experiences which knock**

us sideways, leaving us wondering what's going on. At moments like these, it's important not to confuse the illness of depression with what we feel when life is dishing out its habitual cruelties. And it's important in school to reassure people that what they're going through – unbearable though it may feel – is almost certainly *not* an illness but is because bad things *do* happen in life, however much we try to protect ourselves from them.

Although people deal with things differently, and although there's nothing wrong with *not* wanting to talk, the opportunity to talk at some stage is helpful for most people. Finding someone who's prepared to listen and help us bear our experiences – however painful they may be – is often what gets us through the darkest days. When the listener acknowledges that what we're feeling *is* awful, *is* unfair, *is* extremely painful and *does* feel as if it'll go on for ever, that's helpful. When the listener panics, prescribes obvious solutions or suggests that we 'keep smiling', that's not helpful.

WHO SELF-HARM

In the UK, one in fifteen young people cut or harm themselves deliberately. Girls are four times more likely to do it than boys. But 'self-harm' is an umbrella term. It's worth remembering that when they're feeling bad, adults are also perfectly capable of harming themselves deliberately by smoking, getting drunk, taking drugs and involving themselves in other risky behaviours. And boys may not cut themselves as often as girls, but they still punch walls, they fight, they run away from home… Whatever form it takes, the behaviour shouldn't be so hard to understand. **Self-harming will always be a way of**

trying to say something, and the job of the listener will be to understand what's being said. It's important to stay calm. Whether they cut or starve themselves, pull out their hair or burn cigarettes on their bodies, a person may already be feeling ashamed and stupid; the last thing they need is someone reacting with horror and condemnation. People don't harm themselves because they're stupid. They do it because, at the time, it makes sense. It makes things feel better. Self-harming might feel like a release of strong feelings, blocked feelings; doing it might feel like a relief, and safer than attacking someone. For some people, self-harming might feel like being in control for a change, like feeling alive not dead, like feeling real.

Self-harming is a communication like any other communication, and people are more likely to stop doing it once they feel that their communication has been understood.

With bellies, breasts and legs, you can't ask to see the cuts, but with wrists and arms you can. And you'll want to see, partly to make sure that the cuts are clean and healing, partly to decide whether or not other people need to be told (some cuts are so light that to tell other people would be to over-react) and partly because the cuts will have been a way of saying something which, at the time, felt unsayable with words.

A student tells you about cutting herself. You look at the (barely visible) cuts on her forearm. You have a few minutes before going to your next lesson. You ask, 'If she saw your cuts, what would your mother realize about how you're feeling?'

Variations on this question can be used in many contexts: 'What did you feel like saying? What would you have said if you could? What were you thinking but not saying?' It feels good to tell these things to another person, saying the things we could never say to our parents, the things that might be wholly inappropriate to say to them. And sometimes we can say these things in ways that would never be possible in real life: with *real* emphasis, using the words we *really* feel.

'I'd tell her that I hate my life!' says the student. 'That I hate myself! That I've got no friends! That everyone hates me!'

Whether any of this is objectively true isn't the point. (Her mother may tell a very different story!) The point is that – right now – it's the student's truth. It's what she needs to say. It's how her life feels. You don't have to point out that she might be exaggerating or that you saw her talking happily with friends outside the school gates only a few hours ago. Letting her tell her feelings will allow her to go to her next lesson more calmly and will mean that she's less likely to cut herself later in the day, having had this chance to express herself verbally.

'It sounds like a really tough situation,' you say, picking up your bag. 'There isn't time to say more now, but let's meet tomorrow. It sounds like things are really difficult for you at the moment.' You're not giving her advice ('Stop cutting and take up a useful hobby!') but you're acknowledging that you've heard the depth of her feeling. You're not trying to change that feeling or rationalize it away.

She nods, pleased, as goes off to her lesson.

WHO WANT TO TALK ABOUT SEX

Most people don't or won't talk about sex, partly because sex isn't the most important thing in their lives! But occasionally sex comes up in conversation. Young people worry about sex a lot (having sex, not having sex) and adults probably worry more than they'll usually admit.

It's important that you're not perturbed or shocked but can allow the other person to talk freely if that's what they need to do. **It's important to remember that anxieties about sex, like so many other things – like money, like drugs and alcohol, like various physical illnesses – will almost certainly be symptoms of more important anxieties:** anxieties about being wanted, about trust, about being attractive, about getting older, about being alone... Helping a person to talk about these underlying concerns will usually matter more than talking about sex itself.

WHO CAN'T SEE THE POINT OF LIFE

'What's the point?' is a very good question. 'What's the point of school? What's the point of exams? What's the point of being nice to people?' Young people ask these questions a lot, and so they should. Most adults don't like to be asked about the point of anything, because it rattles our cages, reminding us of our own questions about life's purpose.

Rather than grab at an immediate (and potentially glib) answer, it's better to applaud the question and questioner. 'Good question! Let's think about it together...'

We spend a lifetime wrestling with these big questions and it's important for young people to be reminded of that. A wide-eyed child might ask 'Why do people die?', or a grumpy teenager might ask 'What's the point of my life?' Supplying them with our own answers (assuming that we have any) is to miss the point. What they might really be saying is, 'There are a lot of things I don't understand and I worry that I should understand by now. Does it matter if I don't understand these things?'

Reliable answers to the really big questions are hard to find. Adults think a lot about these questions but tend not to ask them openly because they too feel that they should have the answers by now. But underneath much of our adult discomfort will lurk the same questions, still unanswered, those most important questions that children and young people ask: 'Why am I here? What's the point of my life? Why must I die?'

As long as we're not afraid of our own uncertainty, we'll be able to join other people in talking about theirs.

WHO DON'T CARE ABOUT ANYTHING

There are easier and better paid ways of making a living than working in a school. So for most of us, it's about more than money. It's about children and young people deserving a good education, a fair start in life. It's about them having the potential to go on and lead happy and successful lives. Most people who work in schools believe these things passionately or wouldn't bother getting up for work in the morning.

That's part of the problem. When children and young people (and their parents, for that matter) about whom we care so much insist that they *don't* care about their education or their potential, it challenges everything that we believe in. We're flummoxed, thrown into a spin. We might feel like saying 'How dare you!'

And yet, as part of growing up, children and young people have a right to be disillusioned, to feel like giving up, to lose confidence, to challenge the system. They have the right to be apathetic and defeatist.

'I've had it with school!'

'Because?'

'Because it's pointless! Because it doesn't help you! It just stops you having any fun!'

Arguing with this point of view and explaining that, in fact, school offers great opportunities is pointless. You're not arguing with an intellectual point of view: you're arguing with a feeling and feelings won't shift until they're understood. They can't be rationalized away.

'So you feel like giving up sometimes?'

'Not just some times! *All* times!'

'I can see why school would feel pointless if you're feeling like that...'

As listeners, we need to be clear with ourselves about how much we have personally invested in children and young people. How much do we live vicariously through them? How much do we laud their potential, knowing that ours is limited now by time and opportunity? How much does their negativity incense us because they're failing to live up to the dreams we had for ourselves? **Genuinely listening to another person rather than listening to a hoped-for version of ourselves is harder than it seems.**

'I don't care!'

'About anything?'

'Yeah!'

'Okay, tell me about the things you *most* don't care about?'

'Like what?'

'I don't know... Like your step-dad?'

'I don't care about him! I hate him! The other day I was downstairs and I wasn't doing anything but he started accusing me of stuff...'

4

CONVERSATIONS THAT CAN'T BE AVOIDED

WITH STUDENTS

There are times when we have to talk with students who very definitely don't want to talk with us. They may be of concern because of their progress or behaviour or because they've done something wrong. We're obliged to initiate the conversation, and the student knows perfectly well that we have an agenda.

'I need a word.'

'Now?'

'Yes, now.'

Young or old, softly or loudly spoken, we have institutional power conferred on us. The school will back us up. In a confrontation, the school must ultimately win or everything falls apart. So we have the power and students, by comparison, have very little. However articulate and intelligent they may be, they know the bottom line: if a member of staff insists, then the student must give way. For some, this is too much and they grab whatever power is left to them: refusing to speak, running out of the room, shouting and swearing or picking up a chair and throwing it. When feelings of powerlessness become overwhelming, students might do any of these things and more. So we have to tread carefully.

'It's about what happened this morning...'

'What?'

'In English...'

'Yeah? What?'

'Apparently you were disrupting other students...'

'No I wasn't!'

'Your English teacher says you were.'

'Well she's lying then, because I wasn't!'

Defences are erected. The student prepares for a fight...

Students of all ages hate feeling tricked so it's important to be as transparent as possible. Sometimes a softly-softly approach ('I just wanted a chat to see how you're doing...') only makes things worse because the student can see right through it. He knows that he's done something wrong and your protracted friendliness just sounds false. You might start by enumerating his many qualities, but he can't relax, can't listen and talk about things until he knows what the punishment is going to be. So sometimes it helps to explain the punishment quickly and matter-of-factly ('You refused to do as she said and so you'll need to do a lunchtime detention...') if it frees the two of you to get on with the interesting stuff ('...but I was wondering how things are for you at the moment?').

Not many students will accept that they've done something wrong and must therefore make amends. 'It wasn't me!' they'll insist, 'I didn't do it!' However clear the evidence may be that they *did* steal the boy's bag and throw it in the dustbin, they'll insist that there were mitigating circumstances ('It wasn't my fault! He was saying things about me! I didn't know it was his bag! And I didn't mean for it to land in the bin!'). It's as if they're saying in a roundabout way, 'Yes, but my life's really hard, you know! I may have taken his bag but my dad's just left us, my mum's drinking again, someone teased me about my hair on the way to school and loads of other unfair things keep happening to me!' This might sound like someone begging to escape punishment but isn't really. It's a student begging to have his whole life taken into account because, as long as the rules were clear in the first place, students know perfectly well that if they break the rules they must take the punishment. What matters to them more than the punishment is the wider context in which the incident happened and your appreciation of that. Getting sucked into a prolonged debate about the punishment itself means that there's less time to talk about the context. Better, then, to announce the punishment quickly and matter-of-factly if it means that you can then get on with talking about the important stuff.

It's important to second-guess the anxiety behind the behaviour. For example, students will sometimes shout out in class because they want to be noticed. This doesn't for one minute excuse their behaviour, nor does it excuse them from punishment. But in the long run, the anxiety fuelling the behaviour needs to be understood, or the behaviour will simply continue. Behind the behaviour might be anxieties about being insignificant, about being invisible or uninteresting, surrounded by so many other students competing for the teacher's attention. There might be anxieties about a lack of structure in the lesson and a student's rising fear of misunderstanding and getting things wrong. There might be an abiding anxiety about the power of authority-figures and a fear of being crushed by this particular authority-figure. For the student safely established as The Disruptive One In The Class, there might be anxieties about what it would be like to behave well for a change.

We have to respond practically to the presenting problem because rules are rules, but we also have to respond to the underlying anxiety. They'd never admit it but being kept behind at the end of the lesson allows students to get time alone with a teacher. It allows them to be recognized. It ensures that the teacher knows their name and understands a little about them. It's why we sometimes have our best conversations with students when they're in detention because we have longer with them and have them on their own, which is, arguably, what they wanted all along!

However self-destructive or anti-social it may have been at the time, the behaviour always makes sense to the student. Underneath the violence, the swearing, the total refusal to abide by the rules will be an unconscious need for self-preservation. The behaviour will always be a defence protecting the student from some imagined danger. Until we understand the *meaning* of the behaviour and until the student feels understood, punishing him will make little difference. His defences will remain as they were – vigilant, bristling, hostile.

'You swore at her in front of the class!'

'I didn't! But in any case, she was winding me up!'

'How was she winding you up?'

'Blaming me for talking when it wasn't me!'

Extreme behaviours defend against extreme anxieties. If he could, a student might explain, 'When I feel belittled, I act big; when I'm in danger of being humiliated, I humiliate others; when I feel as if I'm losing control, I insist on controlling others; when I feel unloved, I look for people to hate…' The fact that these behaviours might affect or damage other people matters little to the student because the situation feels to him like a matter of survival. At the time, his behaviour seems to him to be the only thing to do.

The way in which we offer our understanding of this matters hugely. Stripping away a student's carefully erected defence ('Ha! I reckon you hate people because you feel unloved!') only makes things worse. We might understand what's driving the student, but the way in which we show our understanding has to be carefully judged.

'It's interesting that you hate other people so much…'

'What d'you mean?'

'Well, we always have reasons for hating people and usually it's because of how they make us feel…'

'Yeah?'

'Like when they make us feel useless or stupid or like we don't matter…'

'So?'

'So perhaps hating other people makes sense? Perhaps you hate them for making you feel rubbish? Perhaps hating them makes things feel better?'

'I do hate people!'

'I know you do. And you'll have your reasons. You won't hate them because you're a hateful person. You'll be hating them because of how you're feeling and probably because of how you've been feeling for a long time.'

Only once the defence has been understood (how it came to be, why it's become so necessary) and isn't being taken at face value can a student begin to temper and amend it.

Typically, we tell students to 'go away and think about what you've done' or 'sit there and reflect on your behaviour'. But many students can't do this. They spend their lives bouncing around, endlessly *doing*. They can't think about or reflect on themselves because no one has ever sat with them and helped them to do it; no one has helped them to understand the connection between how they (privately) feel and how they (publicly) behave. And there will always be a connection.

There's a useful saying: 'What you pay attention to is what you get more of.' If we pay attention only to the symptoms, to the *expression* of whatever students are feeling, we'll get more of the symptoms, more of the expression. But if we can find ways of paying attention to whatever's powering those symptoms in the first place, then we'll find ourselves having more useful conversations.

And sometimes, rather than insist with students that everything is necessarily 'fair', it helps to acknowledge the unfairness of so much that goes on in school. For the youngest students, things are either 'fair' or 'unfair', but as they get older they have to learn that fairness isn't absolute: there are degrees of fairness, kinds of fairness; we can't always get what we want; we can control some things but not others... In fact, life is endlessly frustrating.

The way students experience frustration is important. If they grow up controlled by their teachers and parents, they never learn to control themselves because someone else is always doing the controlling. And if there's no control at all, if students learn that they can dominate everything, then that's no help in the long run either. There are students who still expect either to be controlled entirely by other people or to be in control of everyone and everything around them, furious when they find that they can't actually control their peers and their teachers. Under pressure, some revert to old, childlike behaviours, once again expecting either to be controlled ('Just tell me what to do!') or to do the controlling ('You can't tell me what to do!'). To rage and scream and despair might be a five-year-old's response to the frustration of all this: a five-year-old inside a fifteen-year-old's body sometimes.

The way we listen and respond to the frustration of students – not with fear and panic but with kindness and firmness – will ultimately determine how they respond to frustration themselves. We have to help them to muddle through, tolerating a degree of frustration as inevitable and understanding that – although at times it feels like it – life isn't deliberately picking on anyone.

'But it's still unfair!'

We could respond to this by saying, 'Well, life isn't fair, is it!' but that never helps: it just sounds dismissive. Somehow we have to find a more collaborative way forward.

'It's not fair!'

'You may be right! And maybe nothing's completely fair. Maybe we're all trying so hard in school to make things fairer – you, me and all the other students and teachers – but maybe we'll never succeed? Maybe we'll end up muddling through, getting some things right and some things wrong?'

'Yeah, but it's still not fair that I'm getting the blame when I didn't do it!'

'It's tough when you feel like that, I agree. And you'll do your punishment and it'll still feel unfair, but that won't stop you being a good friend or having a good sense of humour or sticking up for other people...'

WITH PARENTS

In most of our conversations there's a subtext, a difference between what we say and what we mean, between what we say and what we feel. **As listeners, we have to listen for what's *not* being said as much as for what *is* being said.**

You meet with Mrs. Buckland to discuss her son's progress. 'Thank you very much for coming in,' you say as you walk with her to your classroom. 'I appreciate that it can't be easy with all the little ones at home.'

'I've got my sister to look after the kids,' says Mrs. Buckland, thinking to herself, 'This teacher thinks I've got too many kids! She thinks I can't cope!'

'He's a lovely boy,' you say, sitting down, 'full of energy and enthusiasm. And very good at football!'

His mother smiles. 'He certainly likes his football!' she says, thinking, 'She thinks he's thick! She probably thinks I'm thick as well! She'd better back off or I'm going straight home!'

Somehow you have to have the official conversation (her son is falling behind and isn't doing his homework) whilst also listening to the subtext in order to avoid a fight and develop some sort of collaborative approach between the two of you.

'We've just got to get him to concentrate a bit more,' you say, 'and homework's becoming a bit of a problem.'

'Tell me about it!' says his mother, thinking, 'She thinks I live in chaos! She probably thinks I don't care!'

You guess what she's thinking. 'He's lucky to have you because not all children have such supportive parents.'

She smiles, temporarily reassured.

'If I show you his work,' you say, opening her son's folder, 'you'll see what I mean.'

His mother is reluctant to look, expecting to be exposed as a bad parent.

You start by highlighting the best work in the folder but inevitably have to show her the decline in her son's written work since the start of term. You badly want to ask about the holidays ('Did something happen? Did anything change?'), but with Mrs. Buckland now checking her phone distractedly, you decide to leave that for now. Instead you ask what she thinks might help.

'I don't know,' she replies. 'You're the teacher! I mean, obviously I try to help him as much as I can. He knows he's got his homework to do because I ask him every night if he's got any.'

'Has he got somewhere at home where he can sit down and do it?'

Now Mrs. Buckland is convinced that you're criticizing her house for being small and untidy. She retaliates. 'The trouble is that he never seems to have any,' she says. 'He says you don't set it. And to be honest, I've looked in his planner and I can't see any homework written down.'

At this point you could yourself retaliate by telling Mrs. Buckland that the homework isn't written down because her son refuses to write anything and, in any case, can't write very well. But you know perfectly well that the shame of being considered a bad parent haunts everyone and, if you say this, Mrs. Buckland will undoubtedly hear it as personal criticism, driving her further behind her defences and making any collaboration between the two of you impossible.

You decide to retreat. You outline the boy's strengths, hoping that his mother will hear this as praise for herself.

She looks pleased.

'We just need him to concentrate a bit more at those times when the whole class is getting on quietly with their work,' you say, 'and then he can have his reward of football at playtime.'

'I'll speak to him,' says his mother, softening. She puts out a feeler. 'I know it's not easy for him with his dad gone and no man around to show him the way. It's all down to me, really.'

'That must be hard,' you say kindly.

She starts to tell you how hard it's been for the last two years, needing you to know that, despite everything, she loves her son and is trying her best. You listen. You let her talk. You know that supporting her in this way will be an important way of supporting her son and that greater consistency between the two of you will help him to feel more settled and confident. You compliment her on how well she seems to have done under the circumstances. You share a joke together about parents and teachers never getting any thanks and, with renewed determination on both your parts to improve the homework situation, agree to meet again in a few weeks.

WITH COLLEAGUES

You might be a younger, less experienced member of staff angered by an older colleague's behaviour and determined to say something. Or you might be in a position of responsibility, obliged to speak to a colleague about his or her poor work.

It's important to remember that however old and however experienced we may be, our underlying anxieties don't change very much. We still worry about making mistakes, seeming foolish, not being good enough, not being liked. A sixty-year-old colleague might look unperturbed, having cultivated a look of confidence over the years, but underneath these well-established defences will be vulnerabilities.

In all our interactions, we tend to behave in one of three ways – as the parent, child or adult. And the way we behave is affected by the way the other person behaves. So, for example, if one member of staff takes on the role of disapproving 'parent' ('You still haven't done your classroom displays!'), then the other member of staff is likely to take on the corresponding role of helpless 'child' ('I never get the time to do it!'). If one person takes on the role of defeated 'child' ('I give up! It's hopeless asking you to do your classroom displays!'), then the other person will quickly take on the role of critical 'parent' ('Well, you're the one who applied for the deputy headship, so you should have thought about that before you took the job, shouldn't you!'). We slip in and out of these roles so easily because we've grown up with them; they've become part of who we are, and so, when the pressure's on, we retreat into a simple, polarized world of children and parents.

However, these conversations are always unproductive and what we need instead are adult-to-adult conversations. In the role of 'adult', we don't talk up or down to the other person and, as a result, they're unlikely to talk up or down to us. In the role of 'adult', we don't blame or belittle the other person, nor do we expect them to sort out our problems. Rather, we take responsibility for ourselves and expect them to take responsibility for themselves.

In the awkward conversations we're sometimes obliged to have, it's very easy for the people involved – regardless of age – to lapse into a parent–child conversation, but it's important to try to keep the conversation on an adult-to-adult level. The snag is that when we feel that we might be in the wrong, we readily slip into the 'child' role, and when we feel that we're in the right, we slip into being the 'parent'. Fearing criticism, a long-standing member of staff might start a conversation by pulling rank (as parent), 'How dare you speak to me like this about my classroom displays!' yet by the end of the conversation might be behaving submissively (as child), 'I don't think I'm ever going to get on top of all the things you expect me to do!' Neither role is helpful. **Your job is to keep the other person in the 'adult' role and stay in the 'adult' role yourself.**

'Thanks again for meeting with those parents yesterday. Have you had a chance to get your classroom displays finished?'

'Not yet, I'm afraid.'

'I'm sorry that it's yet another thing to do. But we need them finished before Open Evening, otherwise we won't be able to get the classrooms set up and ready in time.'

'I know, and I'm really struggling.'

'It's a tough time of year. But once this is done we can all relax, at least until the next thing on the calendar!'

Sometimes people seem determined to drag us into parent–child conversations. Using the word 'we' instead of 'I' or 'you' is often helpful in resisting this and maintaining an adult-to-adult conversation. Using the word 'need' rather that 'want' can also be helpful. Some people find it useful to preface the difficult part of the conversation ('Have you had a chance to get your classroom displays finished?') with some praise ('Thanks again for meeting with those parents yesterday') which works well as long as the praise is genuine.

In talking with students, parents and colleagues who would rather not talk with us, we need to bear all these things in mind: thinking carefully about how best to deliver the bad news, identifying and responding to the anxieties underlying the other person's behaviour, listening for what's not being said and avoiding parent-child conversations. Everything else is a matter of one human being listening and trying to understand another.

5

WHO LISTENS TO
THE LISTENERS?

Whether we like it or not, our job in school involves listening to people. But unless we're saints, our confidence and willingness to do this will depend considerably on whether we feel that people have listened to us in the past and whether they still listen to us when we need them nowadays.

For many of us, the person who listens will be a friend or partner or family member. But it'll also be important to have someone in school who listens to you, particularly when you're doing a lot of listening yourself. **Knowing that you can go and talk with someone yourself will help you to continue the work when you're feeling overloaded with other people's troubles.** For example, after a particularly charged or difficult conversation where you've been in the role of listener, it might be important to have someone you can talk with about the effect of the conversation on you. The conversation might have filled you with sadness or anger or with a feeling of helplessness. It might have reminded you of painful experiences of your own. Having someone who can help you make sense of your own feelings is a necessary, professional use of time if, in the long run, it stops you becoming jaded and resentful, overwhelmed by everyone else's misery.

Headteachers will want you to know that their door is always open. But talking with the headteacher isn't always easy. You might need to discuss the conversation you've just had with a distressed colleague where that colleague's confidentiality might be compromised. You might worry about sharing your uncertainties with the same headteacher who'll be writing your reference in the future. And, of course, the headteacher's door is often shut through no fault of the person inside.

Booking a time to talk things through with a trusted colleague – even if it's in several days' time – usually works better than searching around, hoping to catch someone for a spur-of-the-moment conversation.

Those listeners who think that they can do it for all of the people all of the time usually end up in a mess! **Because listening is such an important part of school life, the listeners must find ways of getting listened to themselves.**

6 A CHECKLIST

As busy professionals, we pick up a book and immediately turn to the executive summary at the beginning or to the checklist of key points at the end. That way, we don't have to read the book!

The important point about listening, however, is that there are no short-cuts, no simple formulas to speed things up or circumvent the process of listening to our fellow human beings. In schools, it's tempting to prescribe quick solutions on the assumption that these will take the place of listening, leaving us with more time to deal with all the other demands on us.

Behaviour plans can be very helpful and quick solutions do often need to be found. But unless someone's prepared to stop and listen at some point in the process, the danger is that more and more people – young and old – are left feeling unheard and left feeling that the only way to get themselves heard is to behave badly.

Here are the key points I've highlighted in this book:

- When they don't feel heard, people end up acting out their feelings in order to be heard and their actions often have unfortunate consequences.

- Feeling understood is what most powerfully precipitates change in human beings.

- Good listening isn't about how much time you've got. What matters is the quality rather than the quantity of your time.

- It's important to develop a culture where it's normal for people to get heard, but not by shouting louder than anyone else.

- In school, time spent listening has to be boundaried, partly because the listeners are busy people who don't have much time and partly because, even when people are distressed, they have to learn to wait their turn.

- However old we are, taking responsibility for our lives can be frightening.

- When it comes to love and when it comes to time, we can only do what we can do. It's kinder to be clear about time and important to remember that a little can be a lot.

- Whatever the reason and however ill-equipped for the task we may feel, it's not fair to run away from someone in need.

- We worry that we're expected to work miracles, but effective listening is really about one human being trying to understand another.

- As listeners, our first job is to understand. We're unlikely to be able to solve another person's problem. Understanding what it feels like for the other person may be as much as we can do, but that will be an end in itself, that will be an achievement.

- How a person feels will be the most important thing to understand.

- If you pay attention, you can see or hear another person's feelings.

- When you don't understand, it's better to say so.

- It's okay not to understand as long as you're genuinely trying to understand and not jumping to conclusions.

- As listeners, feeling that we can't help or haven't helped is normal.

- As listeners, our priority isn't to fix things but to understand them: we're trying to understand how another person's life feels, how it *really* feels.

- From time to time, the things people talk about will touch you. You might feel sorry for the other person; you might feel angry or sad on their behalf. You might even find yourself crying in sympathy. That doesn't matter. What does matter is that you don't confuse your own experience with the experience of the other person.

- Your job is to hang in there and do your human best, knowing that you can't put parents back together, can't bring loved ones back from the dead and can't stop people being cruel to each other.

- Getting help for yourself is often the most professional, responsible way of continuing to help someone else.

- Rather than ask lots of questions, encourage the other person to tell you the story.

- Say less rather than more.

- When you do ask questions, ask 'open' rather than 'closed' questions.

- Avoid platitudes.

- Effective listening is about saying less rather than more. So if you don't know what to say, say nothing.

- Effective listening means trying to understand, not jumping in with lots of advice.

- It can be very tempting to share your own experience, but be scrupulous with yourself. If it's really for the other person and what the other person most needs from you right now, then maybe. But if it's really to make yourself feel better, don't do it.

- It's usually better to support a person with words rather than hugs.

- When you find someone hard to like, it's worth wondering whether that's because the other person reminds you of parts of yourself that you'd rather not be reminded of.

- Sometimes we can be doing a good job as listeners and yet still people get angry with us. Usually it's not our fault but is probably because we're unwittingly reminding them of the person with whom they really are angry!

- You can't make people talk. Some people are quite unused to talking about themselves; other people simply don't have words for certain feelings.

- Some people find it hard to believe that anyone's prepared to listen because, in their experience, no one *has* ever listened or been interested.

- Some people don't want to talk because they're afraid of what might come out.

- Your first job is to respect the other person's right to say nothing.

- Your second job is to imagine what the other person would say if only she could…

- When someone says that he doesn't know what he feels, it usually means that he's feeling mixed.

- Saying 'I don't know!' can be a way of avoiding difficult questions, but it's also true that sometimes we *don't* know things: we don't know what to feel, what to think, who to trust, what to hope for…

- You can't promise complete confidentiality to anyone because you don't know what you're about to hear.

- Everyone wants attention. There's nothing shameful or abnormal about that.

- Needing attention means needing attachment.

- Needing attention also means needing to be interesting.

- However inconvenient it may be, it's important not to punish people for making attachments to us. For them, trusting anyone enough to make an attachment may be progress, and they'll only be able to move on once they've had enough of whatever it is that they're needing.

- If they trust you enough and if you've got enough time, people will almost always end up talking about their families because that's where everything starts.

- While no one should ever be forced to talk about death (or anything else), the opportunity should always be there to talk with someone who isn't scared, who won't run away or change the subject, who won't offer false promises and won't try to make everyone look on the bright side.

- We all have defences, and we need them. They keep us safe. They protect us from humiliation, danger, uncertainty, powerlessness.

- There's always a reason for the defence, and our job as listeners is to puzzle it out because then we won't take the defence at face value.

- When people begin to talk about their underlying feelings and anxieties, their presenting behaviour begins to change because that way of behaving, that defence, is no longer needed.

- You can't actually stop anyone – young or old – from killing themselves if they're determined enough, but you can try to understand how they're feeling, which often reduces their feelings of isolation.

- Self-esteem comes from feeling understandable to another person.

- Anger is a healthy emotion. How it's expressed is another matter altogether but, in schools, anger tends to be expressed as swearing or violence, for example, when it can't be expressed as words, either because the angry person has no vocabulary for anger or because no one's prepared to listen to the angry words.

- If you can bear their feelings of helplessness, it often frees bullied people to act for themselves.

- It's worth remembering that feeling bullied by people in school (or bullied by school) may not be a person's only experience of bullying.

- Depression and other mental illnesses are real but, at the same time, we have to remind people that normal life *does* sometimes hit us with experiences which knock us sideways, leaving us wondering what's going on.

- Self-harming will always be a way of trying to say something, and the job of the listener will be to understand what's being said.

- Self-harming is a communication like any other communication, and people are more likely to stop doing it once they feel that their communication has been understood.

- It's important to remember that anxieties about sex, like so many other things – like money, like drugs and alcohol, like various physical illnesses – will almost certainly be symptoms of more important anxieties.

- 'What's the point?' is a very good question.

- Genuinely listening to another person rather than listening to a hoped-for version of ourselves is harder than it seems.

- It's important to second-guess the anxiety behind the behaviour.

- Extreme behaviours defend against extreme anxieties.

- Only once the defence has been understood (how it came to be, why it's become so necessary) and isn't being taken at face value can a student begin to temper and amend it.

- As listeners, we have to listen for what's *not* being said as much as for what *is* being said.

- It's important to remember that however old and however experienced we may be, our underlying anxieties don't change very much.

- Your job is to keep the other person in the 'adult' role and stay in the 'adult' role yourself.

- Knowing that you can go and talk with someone yourself will help you to continue the work when you're feeling overloaded with other people's troubles.

- Because listening is such an important part of school life, the listeners must find ways of getting listened to themselves.